Born in Peterborough in Cambridgeshire, England, Alexandra is a Hungarian and West African writer who grew up with a strong interest in the arts. As a child, she had a love of theatre, dance, film and music. Alexandra took an interest in English literature, in particular poetry and lyric writing in high school. At university and pending further education, she was focused on a career, which she successfully started as a musician/artist, especially abroad. Unfortunately, she suffered spiritual trauma after a 'convenient' misdiagnosis and miscarriage of justice, which hampered fifteen years of her career owing to an absence of support/legal help – and was also partially why she turned to writing for some time. It proved to be a profound, though disheartening, learning experience. Alexandra has studied in a variety of places, completing courses both in England and New York, and continues to pursue her interests and work in the arts field in various ways including as a creative artist, and a singer songwriter.

Alexandra Gyasi

AMARYLLIS SKY

A Poetry Collection

AUSTIN MACAULEY PUBLISHERS™

LONDON * CAMBRIDGE * NEW YORK * SHARJAH

A CIP catalogue record for this title is available from the British Library.

ISBN 9781787100190 (Paperback)
ISBN 9781528952323 (ePub e-book)

www.austinmacauley.com

First Published 2024
Austin Macauley Publishers Ltd®
1 Canada Square
Canary Wharf
London
E14 5AA

Thanks to everyone at Austin Macauley Publishers for their help and support.

Table of Contents

World of Keep	12
Foreign Oubliette	13
In the Art of All Fairness	14
The Pendulum of a Sentence	15
Diagnosis	17
False Accusation – The Sentence that Began with 'Because'	18
"Someone's Sleeping in my Skirts"/ (Bison Byron By son)	20
"I'm Only Alive" – Elegy	21
Dissonant Cadence A Room of Ten Choices	23
'More Than This… For Where a Heart Would Hurt Not' (Elegy)	25
Maladious Sky	27
My Mind Journeys Back	29
To Ever Know "Missing People"(?)	30
The Rivers as They Run	32
Hell Wanted More (To Dare Mock the Skies)	33
Part Two	35
The 'Hurt Locker' that Lasts – To Commit a War	37
Bad Medicine ("Voronezh")	39
Man Of Sorrows	40
And He that Carried the Weight of the World	41
You Know My Name/Amara	42
A Heart's Lament	43
Madame Madelene	44
Live and Let Live R.I.P. Thomas Szasz	45
Looking at You, Looking at Me	47
The Other Cheek	49
Confidential Files – The Taste of Your Tears	51

Remember to Be Polite 52

Deeds 55

An Amsterdam an 'Ave' Knew 57

Human Animal 59

Asylums and Wars 60

Would I Wonder 61

Mind Games 62

The Ghost of a Child's Heart (The Coalmines – England) 65

A Minimalist Piece 66

To See What Happens if You "'Damage' that One" 67

The Squirrel 69

The Garden of 'Ever There' 70

The Journalist's Photographer 71

"A Blind Man's French Dog Cannot *Be Blind,*" 71

Reading Alexandre Dumas 74

"A Tale of Homework Scores" (Tick That... Off) 75

I Read Whilst I Wait 77

Marriage and Divorce 78

Let Me Count the Ways 79

Marionettes 80

The Strangest Sky 81

Eliza of Asylums 82

Jail Terms and NUMBERS Ill Defaults – 5+ 6 = 14 'Wrong' 5+6= 14 'Wrong' 84

Tired of Fighting 85

Tired of Fighting (Part Two) Clock Wise? 87

Juanico's Paintings 89

A Room with a View 90

The Many Faces of Freedom 92

Maybe 93

His Shadow 94

The Playground	96
The Letter	97
Another Place and Time in November	98
Something You Said The Ring	100
His Haunting Madrigal – Elegy	102
An Unkindness of 'Heavens' – The Blackness of Ravens	103
War and Hospitality – To Be Attracted to Leaving	104
The Minks	106
Moonlight Serenade	107
The Mind Behind Your Kiss	108
Blues	109
Searching	111
Unbroken Falls (In Relating to the War and Psychiatric Abuse)	112
To Ever Make A Killing	115
The Golden Gardens	116
I Hear Him in the Winter…	117
And the Summer Rains	118
Of Sunday	119
Tell the Suns	120
Oaths and Sides	121
Spectres and Shadows	122
The String Quartet – Bad Dream	123
With You	124
Paint Me a Place	125
(Poem From 'Russian Midnights' – 2014)	126
Pinocchios and Feathers The Windmills of a Mind	127
Aspect	129
'Burned'	130
The Way that I Dream A Salzburg Moon	131
Abandons that Cast Grounds to Sorrow	132
The Circus of the War	133

**Wednesday's Midnight Skies – The Dance
(Loosely Inspired By Nijinsky)** 135

Drowning 137

The Era 139

33 Decembers 141

In the Dark to Spend My Time 142

So I Tend to Believe 143

Meet Me on a Sunday 144

On the Rocks 145

Empty 147

The Hurricane 148

To Miss You – Come Home 149

The Probable Consequences 151

Forever and for Love 152

This Love 153

Before His Back 154

Eternal 155

Tango 156

If Each Deed Is a Prayer 157

They were still catching war criminals in 2018 – 'You were better when you had no money'

Remembering victims of war crimes, and their lost families and lives.

World of Keep

Rains… as they fall
The sun as it would 'dye'
The 'Soul' of the horizons…
An 'Amaryllis' Sky

'Sacred Madonna'
The way you wore blue
The hours as they 'try' one…
What should I do

To earn a freedom
In this world of keep?
So that, memories of yesterdays
Would allow me to sleep

Eventide to dawn
Do the hours steal away
My prayers within this 'world'
…Would they only hear what I say…

The 'dreams' that one cries for…
This nature of pains'
The 'Vault of Skies' each morn
Their 'sinews' and 'veins'…

And auras of the mind
And the grounds 'about' an Oath
Where the truth battles with lies…
To be not strong enough for both

Foreign Oubliette

Facades as they seem
And darkness takes its time
If God was really watching
How could the devil dare to crime?

Political the music
The ways in which to hate
Any 'innocent' cash injection
To ever know a fate

Paralleled hells on another land
How they lay to rest the living
And hatreds and side effects stay the same
There, there's no misgiving.

The files like a 'bell jar'
And their lies of "Oblivion's" mind
'Eliza' to asylums
No raven of kindness

Social politics… animosities
Any 'doctor' with decision
All their 'slow deaths' beside
Hedonistic irreligion

The violence of injections
The bodies as they 'sway'
Until there's no such thing as innocence
For the devil went to 'play'

To try on reasons for a 'bell jar'
'Oblivion's' arms and callous havens
He lies of her… and 'torn' the skies
With the unkindness of ravens

In the Art of All Fairness

To ever fear… a woman?
To fear… to break a heart?
"As you wish to be treated"
In the art…
of all fairness

The Pendulum of a Sentence

Bruises and apples
The rains… and swollen river
Respect is seldom earned by fear
Leaves as they quiver in the storms

Cold anamneses
And unforgiving past?
The memories to a soul
Closed in on me fast

"The rope about a neck
The 'cruel' of the 'mime'
The scars… on my back
On the skin of my 'crime'"

"The many ways to keep a mind
Yet the many ways to lose
The way they struck my head
As 'a beating' would carouse"

"Livid tongues and their nature about
The "brownness" of his skin
Where eyes are the mirrors of the soul
To regard what another has seen."

5 am to midnight
The skies always sober
The pendulum over a sentence…
A child to ask 'when over'?

To wonder of feeling…
For the heart… is a home
To fall to pray… in the blackness of night
… In the Shadows of alone

How many lifetimes haunt a mind… a soul?
The grounds as they would grieve…
The skies as they remind us…
What is left to us to believe

"And… numberless… and unmarked graves
What there was to gain?
The way that 'skin could tear from bones'
Neath the crucifying rain?"

Fallacious trade and a 'capacity of man'
legalities in years left no mystery
The way that 'fragile' conscience could
… another people's history

When 'paintings' are hanging
To ever question why?
The heart as it beats in a chest…
And the reasons there are to sigh

Diagnosis

Did they
Diagnose a war?
Diagnose a need?
Diagnose a slave trade
Of religion, colour,…creed?

Did they diagnose the pain?
Did they diagnose the hurt?
Can they diagnose what's done is done
And still afford a shirt?

Estranging of man
The Hypocrisies and lies
The things that God would ask
And the way a misunderstanding man defies.

Can they diagnose the devil?
And the nature of its hell?
Can they diagnose the kiss of death
And those who cannot tell

Did they
Diagnose a war?
Diagnose a need?
Diagnose a slave trade
Of religion, colour… creed?

False Accusation – The Sentence that Began with 'Because'

This fascinating darkness…
And grounds and how they dare
For the seen and the unseen…
Where suns and moons become unfair.

To regard my shadow… and numb,
Until I can't bear to sense my self
Yesterdays won't be again
The dreams upon the shelf

And how a spirit can fear
Even though it's broken
Why the nature of the skies would leave me
Such a 'funny token'

The sentence began with 'Because'
And devils at the door
I suppose I must have fallen
For I struggled on the flaw.

To ask for the strangest madness
To be under arrest
Would I but close the door from this world
To journey to the next

How low – to wound that with injury
A further hurt to tell
A neglected world under the coldest realm
The shadows how they dwell.

If hell were ever due
Without tears, to cry…
Some hearts… in vain and cold
'The way a nightmare tried me…'

"Where the patient hangs himself
Another cuts their wrists

-    Metaphorical "prosecutions"
-    Their accusations to abyss"

Am I alone not ever lonely
For some things are true
And it's hardly what I asked for
But what am I to do?!

Rainstorms flood the grounds with tears
The airs as they mourn and sigh
The shadows as they play
And tell me not to cry.

"Someone's Sleeping in my Skirts" /
(Bison Byron By son)

Drs. Bison and Buffoon
To dictate a '<u>kamikaze</u>'
For "<u>when all the dead were sane</u>"
Would <u>I sip some sake</u>?

Psychosomatic – addict insane
For the White… Cliffs… of Dover?
The view over a land and it's waters
Psychedelics… und "NICHT sobre!"

Men's 'sudorific fevers'
In a house of… ILL repute
Funny of Mr. Doctor
To not diagnose or compute.

Drs. Psychopath and Demented
Their ecstasies and apostacies!
To nail in their minds man's odd and slothenly books.
For like a type of 'telekinesis'

Body kleptomania' and injection
The 'body of a nut' as it shook?!!
And then another's section in a rocket
Had an 'aerial' 'look'

My 'delicate antennae'
And thus, To "force my hand"
Not a brown cardboard box…
Called the "One Night Stand"

The tablets of war…
Which commoner was to know?
No grandfather to say 'nay'
And So far from Doctor Zsivago

"I'm Only Alive" – Elegy

(Hunter is used in this context – in place of demon or devil –
'hanta' in Hungarian – a fib)

And the somnolence of these sentences
The earth falls 'a round'
And endlessness of days now,
In visions and sounds

I fall and fall
Into the arms of the snow
My heart becomes cold
From the grounds and their knowing

What the skies don't forgive
The 'hunter's' 'high' and 'low'
For a stolen religion
As I rest in the snow.

The 'end of the world'
The way it finds us
When hells have their eyes
And how they denied us

Shadows and dreams
The way that they daunt
Mazes of candles
Lost prayers as they haunt me.

The daze of the days
The earth 'falls around'
So 'take a bow'
The somnolence of theses sentences

The circus of watching
A heartbreak then !
Sorrows as they gravitate
To 'walk it off' again !

For a crime of broken hearts
And a golden shadow sells
Downward spiral hours
The prisons of many hells.

To fall apart
But to 'fall' a part?
The skies as they pass
Their Knowing and Art

Dissonant Cadence
A Room of Ten Choices

Ordeal and the devil's consequence…
An inferno … fools can feel?!!!
To ever dare to think
The pain is not real

Summers would burn
The winters too cold
Each heartless December
The watch of the ' hold'.

I, the 'sleepless' of sleep
Alive for I wake
The place of abandon
No rest for my sake.

The earth as it circles.
The suns as they should
Would I wish for a world
Where man was essentially good

As though enemies were allies
For the hours behind eyes
In a game of puppets and dictators
What psychologist of the skies?!

Drastic minds
Foolish impatience
To not 'correct the answer'
…So, the dissonant cadence

The Prince of Darkness a 'teacher'?
The netherworld's veranda
Political the music
To carouse each propaganda

And of-course there's no hell?
The blind cannot feel?
To ever dare to think
The pain is not real…

Intellectuals… sadistic crimes
To 'go and come around' again
Complex experiments… assassinations
When, simple, the rain

Chilling minds
The deeds of good liars
Pathological hells
Indiscriminate fires

For given wars and slave-trades
And what is done is done
Devils and their morrows
And how they still have fun?

A room of ten choices
Which one to chose
Memories as they beckon me…
…Which one to muse?

'More Than This... For Where a Heart Would Hurt Not' (Elegy)

Loosely based around, inspired by, Ruslana Korshunova R.I.P.

Saturnine 'falls',
'For a memory is well.'
To wish to have the heart to sleep…
But too "tired" from the hell.

'Sombre… a reflection…
A heart cannot deceive (itself).
And a mind within its labyrinth'
And… one could 'ask to leave'…

The sound of burning candles
The world about one's ears…
The world within a mind
In the shadows and Your tears.

"The way that she walks…
and the sound of a Church bell
Life about the city lights…
Like 'Butakovskiy's waters, her hair as it fell."

An 'amnesia…to 'fall'…
For the sullen are so well?
To acquiesce to 'rest'
For "invisible" the hell.

To close the only door…
From memories on the shelves
The storeys… for a story
What 'soles'… bring on themselves?

Torments and scenes
A 'side' beneath a steeple
And so it is never right
To break the hearts of people.

The evidence of deeds…
For knowledge Is so well
Does the world turn after suffers
Like "Butakovskiy's waters, her hair as it fell"

"It's not good to be too strong…
yet, only the strong survive.
To ever take chances…
For where a heart would hurt not…"

Maladious Sky

Discontentment and unrest
To tell me where I'm from
Should he be alive
Would he know that I am gone?

Innocence and it's nature
The passing of each season
To ever read the skies…
Then papers of politic – man's excuses and 'season'.

Foreign body and asylum
A 'dark pain' in my chest
Anxieties at the borderline…
War and it's gormlessness

The sky above malady or opinion?
Suffocating despairs
To sit alone in the darkness
Until cold and lonely, the airs

Their bloody victories… another's agonies
A ghost left bereft
A world that breaks in hearts
Until no hope is left

Oh… the burning hells of the sun
And such madness 'neath the moon
To always love the rivers…
When skies are gone too soon

Shadows and their *movements*
To wonder of a Name
What war criminal would mar an age
To not wonder of the game

And the drugs estrange a weary heart
For there is no place like home
Side effects and nightmares
That leave some… alone

To read through eyes that can no longer see
Their complex opinions and decision
In foreign tongue the lines
As they filed for a prison

Which prosecution's heartlessness?
Frustrations as they tore
Enemies and wars
A vigilance, and not a paranoia saw

My Mind Journeys Back

And am I too tired
Too tired to sleep
My sorrows dictate
As I breathe and I weep

The weight of the world
And a memory's scars
I goodbye the (grace of the) day
And walk neath the stars

My worries as they gravitate to
A place of no return
And what could be left of me
I dare not discern

There is no peace
And the silence is lonely
For when a heart breaks
It's a one and an only

And my travelling mind remembers
…Of oblivion's skies
And shadows as they haunt until
I'm afraid to open my eyes

I put out the lantern
The room is left dark
In the depths of a night
Alone in 'Noah's Ark'

And what could appease
This hell and it's round
Life kicks me high
Or life brings me down.

To Ever Know "Missing People"(?)

Sharp betrayals in a back
My 'ghost' would walk the halls
The place of "hell's' abandons"
Where no one hears the calls

To only harm the Spirit
But 'not the one they drink'
Their 'drug' plundered my veins
'I am, therefore I think'

Before the Back of God
The crime of stealing lives
The cold screaming asylums
A Sunday's shadows with their 'knives'

A 'bed' assault on 'a clinical depression case'
Without strength to escape the 'jail'
Elsewhere… another would kiss their husband
So… to 'derail' a woman…

Horrors and slaveries…
Another's Sundays (and) Freedoms of will
The shadows of a heart
Her being not an il

Where esurient the devil
The victims… the proof?
The envy of another's sanity
For the skies and their truth

A place of slow murders…
Where one is to learn
Man's lies and hypocrisy…
And that suns are free to… burn.

The place where it SEEMS no God…

They mar an age with hypocrisies
What thing? Believe the devil?
What sighs hearts to temptations
The 'Faith breaker's' hungers revel.

The awareness on any street
And years it was allowed
The world of that 'behind bolted doors'
The skies that cry out loud

The Rivers as They Run

The shadows about a cross
To believe what I see
To think therefore I am
To be or not to be?

The seen and the unseen
Is what is done really done?
Will what will be really be?
The rivers as they run

To ever thank the skies above
For when the war cares to stop.
When God finds children missing
Is it lonely at the Top?

Charades and games of strategy
The 'Laws' to any game
Constant … the skies, and…
The Truth remains the same

And so, is Nothing as It seems?
For the rains that have fallen
Let hell not seek a soul
To cast another war on

Hell Wanted More
(To Dare Mock the Skies)

"Win! Mock Me again
Wait for the sun… as it yields
Injure My injuries… laugh at My hurt
Mock Me again for your (political) 'fields'"

Pull closed the curtains
Close every door
I've seen enough
I can't bear anymore

The sentence of devils
Stories of war
Frozen the era
Their damns of a Law

They enter a room
For the Angels to leave
In the rot of an era
What is left to believe?

The golds of a hell
Shine like vain imitations
The prosaic madness
War's 'rewards' and decorations

Cold meditations
Assassins to walk
A mind occupied
With political talk

Possessions and bribes
And silenced alarms
Machiavelli and cruel…
To live and let arms

An anarchy's hatreds
Oblivions roar
Another soul thrown
To the hells of their core

Excuse me for damning
the 'distraction' that they chose
But to win just to win
When they win but they lose

The anthem of a hell
To hide another prayer
As they raise a glass to victory
For hatreds… to carouse the 'err'

The devil and it's shamelessness
Oh, the bloodshed they told
A man shot five times in the back…
The borderline… cold.

Dark – the games linger
In echoing halls
To ration themselves
With a battle of 'falls'!?

Part Two

To offend the religion we love
FOR DARKEST ORDEAL AND SCREAMING
The Dis-chord of the days
Where squalid…the dreaming

'Win! Mock me again
Wait for the sun… for it yields
Injure my injuries… laugh at my hurt
Mock me again for your political 'fields'

A father… A skeletal figure
Stained… in (war's) blood
A child as he watches
The rivers as they flood

Dissonant days
A war beneath a reign
In the madness of a nightmare
What is a shame?

…The obliquity of war
Not a thing could condone… it
For the Grace of God
To dare to 'disown' it

To pillage with the orders to a heartbeat
Each a victim to the hell
As if the 'nag' for it tells a politic cheated
(for) Another tired soul to sell

War and money…
For how could you deny
The net worth ends that justify means
And any devil's ' slice of the pie'?

The playgrounds of hurt
And heinous the dream
As they bury each scene
With each heartbreaking sin.

Where victories are bloodiest wounds
Another Amen?!
Until out of the sky azure
We are mourning again

Excuse me for damning
the hell that you chose
But to win just to win
When you win but you lose

The 'Hurt Locker' that Lasts –
To Commit a War

(It is) not good for the heart to anger
And some would know this well
War's chaos and disorder…
Life become a hell

To commit a war
To watch the ' 'Son' go down'
And, 'Am I worth saving?'
In this place of no sound?

The mourning as it breaks the storms
Unto Sorrow… and the living
God's anger and it's sanity
For war was there for giving?!

And if hearts are 'sighed' to temptation
The denials of crimes against the sky
To regard a garden's fallen willow tree
And a lonely alibi

To deny what they know
The jails it casts
The way they break in hearts
And the "hurt locker" that lasts

Another cash injection
And it's license then to kill
"Arbeit macht frei"
But no freedom still…

Any falsity's power…
Eerie and odd
The cruelest of things to dare…
To hide a man from God…

For man was ensouled
And the morns are sometimes sad
The angles from a sky
And socially accepted madness

Where man's wrath casts in orders
To give a hiding
Away from any Sunday's peace
Regard the soles beneath us…

The fault is *always mine*
And if forgiveness is divine
To live with the self **and the nights**
Then that of the heavens which judges the crime.

Cold alienations
Nightmares as they feud
In its lack of imagination
The devil's fantasies were crude

Bad Medicine ("Voronezh")

Laws and Commandments
How… they are
Felt
To be taught to 'read'
For the 'agenda' I was dealt.

To master emotions… with heartbreak?
Oppressions before a Sky
The nature of dreams
And lonely alibi.

St. Petersburg' Skyline
Neath the shimmering rain
But…
To beg at another 'door' in another town
To hope that they were sane

A cold 'hand' dealt
And so, minutes as they passed
Life perhaps is short…
But how long… does it last?

How the problems of one place
Follow to the next
The "'doors' would keep on closing"
My dying consciousness more vexed

Politics and treasons
The seen and the unseen
An inhuman kind of tory
A lifeless life support machine.

Man Of Sorrows

The 'Game' of Agreed
The Creed of a 'Game'
The Tears of the Rain
They always remain

Fires roar
The beauty of your path
Thine kin un-shy to speak
Thine 'hair' shy of wrath

And He that Carried the Weight of the World

It's funny how sometimes the heart beats on,
Even though it's broken
And how words still have 'breath'
After they're sung or they have been spoken

A mazing mind of thoughts…
About you as you breathe
A chest as it falls and rises and falls
Vulnerable that, which is worn on a sleeve

Where a soul hath journey in the storm…
Leaves with their lines when they quiver
For, to bear, the name of He that carried
'the weight of the world', heavy across the river.

R.I.P.

You Know My Name/Amara

Her feet weep in blood learning the grounds
The dirt track would burden with toll
And stones that dig into and scrape at her skin
Like a journey would 'mock' a soul.

Scarlet stains soak into the parched grounds
The memories for morn where she fell
Early the hour… before the sun burns
'Repenting'… for she has no well.

Silence screams the perils of the path
The wake of those who have fallen
Ophidian venoms… their injury's wrath
The look on her face, so sullen

Of deeds and shadows the world
Each 'has their own shoes'…
The sky above, about her struggled soul
Why everyday, they lose…

And how hurt a heart
Who is to say?
Who dares to judge…
How long is a day

The freedom of freedom
To suffer what we must?
Though what pains the Vault (sky) today
Its somehow hurting all of us.

A Heart's Lament

And who knows what the skies would think
And tears as they are sent
The rain that beats the grounds
Reflects a Heart's lament

Vultures as they circled
Over graves… their sober looming
The airs 'pierced' with screaming
As they homed in with their doom

'Home is where the heart is'
But the home it was not theirs.
An injured soldier neath the Vault of Skies
What vulture's hook'ed bill…it's tears.

To 'assassinate a character'
Scavengers as they tore
To resign the flesh from power
And they must have asked for more

A man's war and merciless fabrication of days
The 'vulture' it becomes
And shadows of the fallen
The scarlet river as it runs

They believed what they wanted to
To then suffer the toll
For once darkness was a mystery
Now it's patronizing dole

"And I am too tired
But Too tired to sleep
My sorrows dictate
As I breathe and I weep

There is no peace
And the silence is lonely
For when a heart breaks
It's a one and an only".

Madame Madelene

(ref. to spell another's name incorrectly)

To bear to feel another day
The 'knife' that scorns a 'back'
To wake up in the strangest room
The midnight-morning black-ness

Thorns about a mind
A cross beneath the stars
'Tribal', then the devil
For emotional, these scars

And the shadows seem to follow
To tell me where I'm from
And to say that I exist
To find out that years have gone

Magdalene's asylum
For the spirits of December
To recall the way they hurt the days?
Then say… 'I don't remember'

Live and Let Live
R.I.P. Thomas Szasz

If I am You
And You are me
The many things
they do not see

If I am you
And you are me
The sunless skies of
My freedom

To cast insults at me for each morrow…
And all that hell could lack.
The way they disgust a mourning
Before my deeply scared back

The weight of the world
The weight of the dead
And, genocides of the slavery
How that was said

To take a 'Book' and read
When days no longer call
Pitiful, the cost of a woman's life
The coldest writing on the wall.

What pounding on paper
'Black and white' the rains
A 'doctor' insults with diagnosis
The lawless nightmare as it gains

In remembering the dead
And scenes of broken law
The 'doctor's' institutional crime
For their hatreds knew before

The wailing of any siren
A person is beaten, neglected
A screaming voice as it tires and calms
An unorthodox world and that (which is) subjected.

The agreements to an injustice
The souls neath the skin that took blame.
To break the Heart of the Skies each time
To wonder of shame

For life is only so long
And what a day is for.
Cold the years of man's thinking, sometimes
Scenes of ruin and broken law.

Looking at You, Looking at Me

(R.I.P. Madiba Nelson Mandela)

The stain of injustice
And slanted imagination.
A flag's cloth once torn
By a conjured segregation

Possessions of politic
The 'colour' another man sees
To edit truths from lifetimes
Disrespectful 'a party's' diaries

One has been given… to be human
Therefore, to have human feeling
Rains fall upon the 'skin' of the Ocean
The sow of the skies and a dealing.

The sound of one's own soul to judge
What a prison really is
When one sees the Face of God –
So what do they miss?

To regard a cross and prison
As a stranger's window and pain.
My brother, 'How our eyes see freedom differently,
Beneath the falling reign.'

Twenty seven years…and loud an injustice
In the name of a marred age it seems…
An 'allowed' to disavow the peoples' liberty?!
For the moon… On High as it engages dreams

There are the grounds
The Sundays, and the men
There are the heavens
With the education they are given.

The sands of time, and the lines on hands.
Then the lines to cross to understand
A sentence is an ambiguous thought
For simple a line as one man writes upon a land?!!

Deliberate the skies
For His tears touch the rains
Seeing is believing,
And so, the blood shed from His veins.

Dear a homeland amidst accusing shadows
I carried my soul neath a battle of skies
I carried my heart through the trials that were given
I carried the woes, for were given my eyes.

I carried the sounds as they lied through Your
Laws
I carried the burdens cast
I carried the lines as were given my hands
I carried a pain that would last.

One has been given… to be human
Therefore, to have human feeling
The way that the sun beats down on the heartland
The sow of the skies and a dealing.

The Other Cheek

(ref. 'Vault' = 'Vault of the Skies')

450 years…and cruel the hours…
To dream in the skin of scolded sentence
As if the rains could beat a back so,
Days of a sarcasm and 'repentance'.

"Win… mock Me again
Wait for the sun – as it yields…
Injure my injuries – send more pain to
pain
'Burn' me again For your fields…"

"Rabid, 'inferno' as it once 'learned'
My skin A man cast to the fire
"My 'actions', and such consequence
My breath until… *it tired.*"

When rivers ran as scarlet…
And, The water it was thick
A Broken Law made memories… of 'morrows'
And how they always made me sick

The envy of freedom
What man? What creed?
The nature of lashings
To watch as I bleed

5 am to midnight
450 years…
'when over?'
Eventide. *to weigh … the graves …*
in rains…
before the 'drover'…

The walk of a man… speaks
And life, an education
Whatever makes us human?
The years of trepidation

And, was it savage… the liberty…
To Blind To beat
To apprehend To cast a Brand…
To 'scar' To kill… In efforts to offend

"The chains about my ankles
Their harshness on my wrists
…rains as they fall over my eyes
Beneath the skies they often missed."

"Win… ! Mock Me again
Wait for the sun – as it yields…
Injure my injuries – send pain to my wounds
'Burn' me again for your fields!!!'

And "may"… injure the "May"
Injure the Mays of my freedom
Night turns to day… Day turns to night
Memories held by a Vault, and it's wisdom.

When rains cross horizons,
And fall over the Seas
To pray on the rocks,
Neath the skies upon His knees…

Confidential Files –
The Taste of Your Tears

The experiments of war
As if an abyss were nigh…
To doctor any file…
To watch impatiently as people die

To mention war. The darkest day
'To cause in trepidation
And of its garish and bloody writing on the wall
Would they lack imagination

Premeditated death tolls
Forgiveness still divine?
And melancholia compliments sin
When the lawless cross the line

The 'golden ball' at sunrise
To regard the day as it's dawning
And the alter ego of the heavens in storms
The shadows in angered mourning.

The veneer of circumstance
The Skies and that which they see
The Empyrean as it watches
…What the world doeth with its freedom…

Remember to Be Polite

(ref. "God believes in people, or do people believe in God?"

quote taken from film (Dan Brown), "The Da Vinci Code"

"What a 'colour' I have passed
To ask how long… a day could last?"

God believes in people
Or people believe in God?
The Skies as they regard
The way that souls are led.

Regard the soles beneath us

Where the patient hangs himself
Another cuts their wrists

- Metaphorical "prosecutions"
- Their accusations to abyss

The coldest of psychologies
Somebody's 'doctor' knew reverse
A book of how to starve the soul
Assisted by a curse!

To herd them just like cattle
To ever ask for more
People dragged back screaming
Through a weighted door

Hails blanche as doctors' coats
The mists were ever haunting
How a hell could 'cry for more'
Neath their formal damns and taunting.

Educated and criminal hearts,
Low form of humour
The archenemy had conscience?
Another had alchemy and rumour.

To speak ill of the dead
In psychiatric terms
So read another proof
Their devil and it's burns
For if the devil had a heart
It's mechanic not to care
The conundrum of the war
And the madness that is there.

A boat as it struggles
– it sails unfurled
Beneath the cruel weather
And the weight of the world

A darkness as it 'thrived'
For what the daytime saw
Their words as they rang
Their convictions like a war

A land of no Sundays?
Or soul there to find?
The asylum off Church Lane
A mind doctor collecting money pretends to be blind.

Picture frames of suicides
To only break the broken
The horror of the exiles
The devil and it's token

The 'kidnaps' of mothers, brothers
Women and their children
Fathers sisters strangers slaves
And any politic – that rewarded them

Godless diagnoses
Their 'propaganda' (spread) like a 'leprosy'
The madhouse handed down stories of hell
the moral infirmity of that ecstasy

Psychopathy of accusations
A fantasy thinking of devils
The paintings in those prisons
Their malignancy on many levels

Each time to speak ill of the dead
Diagnosis judgement decision
The madhouse handed down stories of hell
In assassinating derision,

An unkindness of asylums
Ravenous the 'envy' of another's freedom… (To cause choler).
What devil's 'carrion' of the world as it turns
The inertia and the dolour

God believes in people
Or people believe in God
The Skies as they regard
The way that souls are lead.

Deeds

A 'bed' violation on a melancholia case
Without strength to escape the 'jail'
Elsewhere… another would kiss their husband
And so, to 'derail'… a woman

Each to their heart
As the world is to its turn
And how we don't always
Choose what we learn

Regardless of forgiveness
For time has its role
Nothing compares
To the loss of the soul

Man and his shadow
Or a woman of questionable deed
The skies as they regard
The grounds and their creed

"Dull the shadows
Rains as they pound
The days as I roam
If I am not lost I am not found

But… errs as they vex
As hours prey upon my sex
To climb out of one problem
To falter to the next

Blackguards… hypocrisies
The earth's conscience to trust
To ever envy capacity or freedom?
And a shameless and strange injustice.

Hell and it's forget me nots
Days when they are 'played'
Where? The love of Sunday?
Was I not curious for the jade

When the shades of the skies would anger
Do they love to fate?
The shadows in the storms
As I wonder through a gate."

Each to their heart
As the world is to its turn
And how we don't always
Choose what we learn

An Amsterdam an 'Ave' Knew

(21st century – social decline – anti abuse – e.g. anti brothel sentiment)
(inspired by a Romanian girl who was kidnapped by a 'boyfriend' and sold to
work in Amsterdam)

To brag… of soullessness?
Malevolent and… illiterate fools.
To ever know what Love is
When they go break all the rules.

'Faces… and their demons
With nothing to lose
Their freedom! in a 'joint's' café?
Their puerile carouse.

To walk past a Churchyard
The nature of groom
But the district of light
A district maroon…?

Men of 'that description'
And a woman looks away with her clutch
Until when man wonders of Heaven
He wonders of too much.

When each devil revels the hindmost
The coldest game in the book
Her labours… in a window
Amidst a world of many crooks.

And questionable intentions and 'eyes'…
For it's rude to stare…
Sunday's convictions
What a darkness dares to dare'

Temptation and 'dangerous teacher'
The devil can be staunch (to a hell)?
The 'lace' of a snow white wedding dress
And the Church bazaar of carte blanche.

The force to mar an age
'Another stranger by a bed'
And pray, as you did
The thieves that disrespected the "dead".

Show me the heartland
A soul become pathetic?
A prosecution's witness
And an era's lost ethic

Take for instance… a life?
The shadows that gazed
A war and fool cast those sarcastic
Blue murder days.

The coldest game in the book
Beneath skies of black and blue
Lonely celebrations
The Amsterdam an 'Ave' knew.

To dismiss and disparage
What man takes… to give?
Where darkness is unsafe
What kind of world to live in?

Emasculating and amoral
The coldest game in the book
Her labours… in a window…
The world and it's crooked.

'The 'leaves' on the trees
Prisons and wounds
Alone… a loan
Neath the knowing Moons

In a world of consolations
People and their 'masks'
The tourist as he window shops
Another Sunday, as it passes'.

Human Animal

To look in the mirror
What do I see?
So to seek (another) human animal
To be friend and company.

Asylums and Wars

Foreign asylum
Façade and will
Borderline agendas… deceptions
The many ways to kill.

Stories that destroyed mothers, brothers
Women and their children
Fathers, sisters, strangers… slaves
And anyone else that occurred to them

Narcissism and psychopathy
Like a fantasy thinking of devils …
To 'doctor' any will to live
A hell on many levels

Violence and formal injections
The bodies as they 'sway'
Until there's no such thing as innocence
For devils as they play

To premeditate detentions
To interrogate before a war
The horrors of asylum chains
The injury that people saw there.

Saturnine Saturday
Silent the lay (of the countryside)
Tomorrow would tell
The time of a Sunday

The old asylum just down Church Lane…
Souls and their eyes.
What man did for money
The things to realize.

Stealing wills at will
The hell on many levels).
And narcissistic psychopaths
Their vow of poverty as the devil's!

Would I Wonder

Gashes on the mirror
Reflections of the toll
Bruises on the picture frame
The injury to any soul

When time, takes it's time
And days become too cold
When nights are blind with storms
The story they unfold

Pictures and feelings
On another's land
The patience of the shadows
How they understand

The hungers of the 'faith breaker'
A forbidding darkness as it deals
The nature of a bad dream…
The bad dream as it reels.

For the nature of shadows
That are 'safe in their skin'
Neath the fire of Your midnight skies
As I wonder where I've been.

Mind Games

When a crime scene is too clean
What 'doctor's;' sterile tools
When flagrant the 'evidence' before the Skies
To witness the devil and its fools

The hairs on a head are they numbered…
Though seem, numberless *the days*
To generally prefer to wonder of something else
For, the 'wilderness' … *of mind games*

A watch… and it's hands move…
The things that people say
What you don't know cannot hurt you
But on any given day

Woes and sorrows as they sketch a day
For grounds sense… as the shadows play
To wonder You would tell the truth
To wonder why the skies are grey.

Until… am I tired again
And my spirit dares not look
For the memories that a darkness left
Had 'one hell of a right hook'.

Experiments after the slave trade
If allowed so to deed
To admit, they were human bodies?
To wonder of a creed

When a man is ensouled
What should he not sell?
For to ask of what is Sacred
But the kiss and tells of the devil.

The mind… as it moves
Slowly to a single thought.
To consider the heart and the soul.
For the things that are felt… and not taught.

To claim 'victories' could take in lives
That 'solution' could only, get colder
Deeds iniquitous and disrespectable
The excuses of ages get 'older'.

To war at all… a foolhardy 'devil'
Politic and infantile lies
Unsympathetic… the hours they dare force
To the 'Stomach' of the skies

It's 'doctor's' bizarre mental crises
Ephialtes as they linger
A decision and it's pride or sloth…
But be advised to 'not point a finger'

A mind for blinds on windows
Revolving clockworks… locks
The dark coat of a gunman
Waiting at the docks

Each cold assassination
In the cruel and wrath filled restlessness…
And the heartfelt reasons to cry…
Until sad times are the best.

For what of happy memory
When it brings one too much pain
And where countless the dead
To say – another hath gain?

Prisoners of war…
Drugged and injured –for what they knew
The bias of a hospitality's lawyer
Another's devil flew

To war at all but Thou shalt not kill
Perhaps, a politician's dalliance
Verily to say of madness then?… as
Lives hang in the balance

For the Bazaar in a Temple
To be that of selling the soul?
As confessions dwell beneath the skies
The tragedy of the toll.

Verily… to say of madness then
A war…or cruel change of 'story'
Calamitous the devil
And it's… 'To be or not to be'…

A madman Is a sinner
To walk into that fire?
The strangeness of irreligion
For how or why one views a liar.

And to report 'the dead. as expected'
… the likely outcome and sin of the war
To dare plot again tomorrow
For a world of Broken Law?

Witness' diaries stained with blood
By the sweating summers of agitation
The flatlines of 'a cruel crime'…
To lack imagination

The Ghost of a Child's Heart
(The Coalmines – England)

Overtired eyes
His arms worn, and thin
'Downcast and bruised
And the bones 'neath his skin

And silhouettes of slaveries…
The labours of any child
Darkness brings it's nightmares
So nights are seldom mild

How to break a mother's heart
A lantern and it's gaze…
Her woe ….he's often coughing…
Monotone the mime of the days

The 'monsters' of the coal mines
How they often haunt
The scare of morrow's memories
As they undermine and taunt

The dreams of a child
Hardships and time
The bread on the table

To die for… in the mine

A Minimalist Piece

THE SHADY WORLD OF SOME MEN

"Morris?"…

"Yes Doris".

The one who was playing footsie at the luncheon with one of the guests behind his wife's back."

How I loathe
Lotharios
And cradle snatching dears
The err how it grows
From their nose (knows) and their (f)ears.

To See What Happens if You "'Damage' that One"

(ref. origins of psychiatric culture were based on Western philosophy including
in Russia/ Give to the world the best that you have…etc)
(quote by Helen Steiner Rice)

Give to the world
The madness you have
The madness returns

Caucasian the madhouse
"Facts they care to omit"
(sometimes) Ruthless people with Eeyorish jobs
Like a dog – returns to its vomit

"Car…toon patients
They shatter and they break
Until they are left with…
No reason to wake"

A heart and it's witness
The foreign asylum and it's beds
To desert their own brethren
To wait until they're dead?

What tourism industry
What curious hospitality
The sightseeing odyssey
To lack cordiality

The stories destroying mothers, brothers,
Women, and ther children
Fathers, sisters, strangers… slaves
And anyone, that 'occurred' to them

A psychiatric section,
So, youth is wasted on the young
The net worth of the doctor
The patient as he hung (himself)

"Car…toon patients
They shatter and they break
Governmental escapades
"Have you taken your medication?"

Their… "Economical with the truth"
For to break in hearts is minor…?
Very impotent manners
So, I read at the Spanish diner…

To plan a 'breakfast'
Hospitalities deceive
To repeat false accusations
Until they are believed

The quack was a quandong
Waiting for may
Memories that last for years…
And just one more day.

He Whose Father dictates the hour
The Skies and their Regard
And do the Angels serve one another
And the Truth that they doth guard.

The Squirrel

The birds as they would sing for Spring
The season in its zest.

A squirrel as it gathers nuts
My mind I ask be blessed!

The Garden of 'Ever There'

When people have 'angles'
Neath the suns as they 'bear'
The scenes where you've been
When you've 'never been there'

Imagine…

The Journalist's Photographer
"A Blind Man's French Dog
Cannot *Be Blind,*"

(no offence or criminal provocation is meant by this work)

"Go to talks
Sip some tea
Another day
123…"

The alpha dog as he saunters
Political the fog
For man is a hero?
(And I like to walk my bulldog).

The speech was cogent
The lies at the hub
One politician's poor guise
At the "Gentleman's Club"

Follow then, a rather 'gormless joy'
The infidel mind in his dealing
Reflections as they played
In the mirror on a ceiling.

And to stay faithful to anything
The skies as they sigh
The fresco as it watched
Without batting an eye.

Watching the sun go down
The confusing task of the war
To carouse with a few 'friends'
To go to work once more?

Unwonted the gaiety to his manner sometimes,
It always was clear.
His wife checks his tie…
"How are you dear?"

Next, "What 'New Clear weapon'? Which 'sober'?"
"Shambolic"… then, what is illegal?
How to say "I have a dream…
That I'm the archfiend 's equal?"

To read a Book on Monday
To need an arm or crane?
To borrow mischief from the devil
And seldom sum a shame

A slave… to the rhythm of politic
Tight corners, as they're 'fed'
Even scrupulous a hedgehog displays it's spikes
To ever watch where the world is lead…

For, foul… the damns of the devil…
And a man's soul is manned
To what does one pledge an oath…
When the darkness can take hand

Halfwits of foolish cause alone
For 'expensive'… the crockery
To read the Book by Sunday
For disrespectable the mockery

To hell the people fallen?
To insinuate a fate?
As he sits for supper
Forsooth, in sin he ate

"Go to talks
Sip some tea
Another day
123"

The sky like 'ceiling'
The heart is of feeling
Not cold…
And political chains.

Go take a Book and read
And have some human feeling
The vault as it remembers
The sky like a ceiling.

"Go to talks
Sip some tea
Another day
123…"

Reading Alexandre Dumas

Actions are souls
The things that they say
Reading Alexandre Dumas
In a Cuban café.

"A Tale of Homework Scores"
(Tick That... Off)

(ref. Charlie – name/ colloquial for cocaine)

Man and his life's bitter cup
A sky's 'back' would bear a scar?
If the earth becomes...' emotional'
Then that "victim" won't get far?

Reliant on natural, and nuclear disasters...
Dishonest measures and their weights
An era so consuming
The game "tectonic plates"

It's a suspicious jungle out there
"Decorum" and it's ways
The painting is wonky and tilted
But it's straight in the 'realm of the days'...

Man and his 'crutch'
The way that he struts
Regard how the cappuchin
Chews on some palm nuts

What heavy criminal record?
The shrink, leaves 800 lbs?
A weight in illegal drugs and wartime bier.
Countless baby booms and rounds

The trance of bulging biceps,
And bank accounts galore
Whilst witnesses were cast to confessional "asylums"...
Behind a bolted door (in...''not a very helpful society)'.

Fauler Smith ! Bist du verruckt?
Mary and Josephine travelled?
Thou shalt not judge the experiments in chemistry class?
What mystery unravelled!

Move to the left …
Right
Mmm… right…

'Charlie' can mar! '… 'Charlie can ma?'
Ja …In gay abandon, the doctor's 'transmitter-transPONDER!!
And..WHERE were Randolph and Jim… on the germinating streets?
The 'tired of treadmill – serf-responder'.

Then Mister Business 'Cold Cash'…
Bad to the bone
What he hides in his brain
The erroneous zone

I Read Whilst I Wait

Drunken am I
Mine heart in mine head
Her turbulent 'breast'
Over something I said

I prayed her forgiveness
The roses were red
Yet still, she is vexed
And lonely my bed

Mine ear to her door
As though nothing could tame her
Caterwauling is she
There, alone in her chamber

Her desires by sundown
I anticipate
Reliant her appetence
I read whilst I wait

"A walking stick to sense the ground
For love, they say is blind
And if you had the strength to see
The sightlessness ye find."

Marriage and Divorce

Marriage and divorce
The empire of fools!
Jocund… be the age
As they make and break the rules

The heart and it's chambers
It's a monumental epic
Each simpleton's commotion –
The bed and that pandemic

Human animals and instinct
The grounds as they gaze
The heavens seem ambivalent
The footage of the days

Love gets under the skin
Like a needle (that's) hypo dermic
Hail hot water bottle
Else my bed be hyper-thermic

And of love and religion
Would I realize a drink
Whilst an episcopal decorum
Would deliberate and think.

Notes
Seek and ye shall find
Remember to be blind
Love is in the heart
Seldom in the mind

Let Me Count the Ways

Roses are red
Freesias are
Free and blue
The 'illness' of love
On the Church pew

A bothersome burden
The pains in my neck
Let me count the ways
That I am left a wreck

It haunts my concentration
It's 'harassment ' stirs my wrath
An unrepentant inconvenience
A boulder… to my path.

The oddity of this odyssey
The skies of foolish laughter
A cliff from which to fall
To only tell you after.

Marionettes

The Angels say 'Hello'
They came about somehow
This game of Marionettes
But I don't remember now?

How, I don't feel like dreaming
There's nothing left to see
If blindness loved the blind
But my soul won't let me be

At St. Leander's 'one a.m.'…
A heinous crime it be (to be alone)
So be attracted to leave it
Beneath the willow tree

The place we loved in secret
Now I sit there alone
The way in which I miss you
What God could condone?

The ghosts that dwell in the dead of the night
When skies are just too far
The Law of Heart and the Hallowed
And I wonder where you are.

To feel the rebellions of time
In the motions of the sea
The vault above the grounds
It's Graceful Sanctuary

On a Mount of Sacrosanct
The Temple 'clay pots' talk
And the Laws beside the Golden Seas
The souls would know to
Walk.

At St. Leander's 'one a. m'
A heinous crime it be
So be attracted to leave it
Beneath a willow tree.

The Strangest Sky

And life like a circus
Bitten, and shier
Left in this place…
Where I walk on a wire

Once a day becomes a bad dream…
And memories delude
Reflections as they haunt
A lonely solitude

Eliza of Asylums

Shadows?… they tear at me
And nightmares… they haunt
The rains fall in their soullessness
The way they hurt and taunt.

And now there's nothing left to say
Of slave-trades or of wars
Do not break of hearts
But man's "maybe lives of laws".

Frustrated and tormented calms …
And what I 'get' if I stir…
To stall a woman for the days of a life…
Sedations and 'crashes' and lines that they blur.

And must I turn back unto memories
And play now with their fires?
The request of some heavens
Their wants and desires.

And grounds believe as they wish to
The mystery of their ways
Injustices … institutions
… 'Siberian' days

And night time's estranging 'winter'
And days too cold to bear
Shadows as they linger
How they still taunt my hair

To hit or to strike me
At least, for it shows
But the nature of a sadness
That nobody knows.

Storm clouds cross the skies
The heavens that they mask
And to turn back any gloomy day
A thing one couldn't ask.

The angles of the lunar
Through the verges of a madness
To blame the purple skies
For these shades of angered sadness

Shadows of the rain
play upon the wall
The commanding moods of the thunder
'Catch me as I fall'

The candle we lit in the forest
Our reflections in the lake
The ways in which we dream
And how we don't have to wake

I fall into myself
And remember how we were
The truth and where it leads me
The storms as they stir

Jail Terms and NUMBERS
Ill Defaults – 5+ 6 = 14
'Wrong' 5+6= 14 'Wrong'

The anger in a Temple
The 'vault of the skies' does it hurt
A war, and it's bizarre bazaar
The earth knows it's dirt.

Lives become 'paltry'
And delirious with pain
Sanguine stains on the clothes of the fallen
Bleak the skies beyond the falling rain

Arms and marionettes
Repeated histories sold
Thus, to speak ill of the fallen
Something known …something cold.

Ironic – its only paper
But where the devil rests intention
The root of all evil and…
Deeds too cruel to mention

When dreams turn to nightmares
As they linger neath the stars
To prophesize a war
Then to find there's "death on Mars"?

Offended… each Sunday
The skies of 'black and blue'
When politic becomes as an underworld
The sky of
'Nothing'… to do.

Tired of Fighting

To wear a medium
A bulldog with a jacket
"To light up again
One day, I'll give up the packet."

The first war cast…
Man's fool…A million more
For history repeats the devil's end?
The strangest thing the people saw

To 'nag'… a soldier's heart to kill
With orders, when man was born free…
Where mind is over matter
The Skies that 'shadow' and see

To hell a sub-conscience to that neath a war.
The horrors of that temptation.
To fell the grounds to bloodthirst
Streets of sin and trepidation

"How you make me want
How you open my eyes to oblivion
The strangest thief of heart
It's in how you make me cry."

The violence of the storms
The ways in which they sigh
To ever believe
The way deeds could lie…

What to cry for by a cross
Where the silence is too loud
Grave, To Watch the Sun Go Down (On Your "Shift")
Neath a disavowed
'Blue.'

For the 'firing' in a hell
A barbaric memory and its 'burn'
The weapons of each day's nightmare
That somebody's dying to learn…

Again… not to war.
But the darkness tries the people
Predator, politic and prey
Would skies watch the
"Sheeple"

A Sunday of strange occupation-
A 'hurt locker'… and 'no way out'
To read the constellations
For the consternation and doubt.

What to cry for by a cross
Where the silence is too loud
The tongue of all the prayers
Neath a disavowed
'Blue'?

To (dare) devastate life
For God's warning of sorrow
'seen it once not seen it all?'
To wonder of tomorrow.

Yesterday's skies
Could a heart waste away
For God only knows
In the dark of the day

Tired of Fighting
(Part Two)
Clock Wise?

History repeats
But the devil always 'ends'
Or turn left? Right…
'Right?'
The clown of days war sends.

The slave of things confusing
And of days who can tell
Any impatient decision
And scenes are not well again

To erase a morrow's yesterdays?
For those 'ours' were they dear
To regard the tarnished grounds
Deeds without fear

And all is fair in love and war
But war cannot be fair
To ever fall to trust
A "monster's circus" and it's dare

Melancholy December
The nature of that crime
To remember of war only that
One cannot turn back the time.

Decorations for "Oblivion's circus"
Man's sensational bribes and thought
The way to hide a heart from God
When another war is taught.

To learn by example?
Experiments of war
To detach and lack any empathy
For what a human being is for?

Decorations for "Oblivion's circus"
fantasy and taught
The way to hide God from man
When another crime is taught.

The nightmares on the street
Nostalgias in their ruins
Numberless the demons
Slumber-less the doings

For eyes to acclimatize to
Political offences and "receipts"
Though only to deceive the self
For the devil's inferno and it's heat?

Juanico's Paintings

'To take a 'Book'' and learn
The picture in the hall
The 'hand ' of Juan De Pareja

That painting on the wall.

A Room with a View

Life… and it's scenes
Until Nothing will call
For once you've seen one
You've seen them all.

Memories as they grieve me
I try to run away
But sorrows as they gain on me
Until they won't let me at bay

Tumultuous emotions…
Then the tired 'fall' to calm
The nature of goodbyes
Till they no longer alarm

All was as I left it when
I went back to that room
The sun dimly lit the place
In the cool late afternoon

A New York City view
Windows reached the ceiling
Yet the people on the street seemed far
And I had my own 'dealing'

I sat down on the mattress
That lay upon the floor
No one ever came there
The cold and barren door

All was as I left it
And people seldom change
The nature of the clouds
And how they rearrange

The sun as it shone
The silence as it crept
The solitary room
I was tired though I'd slept

I was tired – it was strange
Too worn out to scare
Nothing to know just that
Life wasn't fair.

I wasn't really thinking
I just stared at the gloom
As if I sensed a presence
In the stillness of the room

The Many Faces of Freedom

His Blood upon the Grounds
That mourn every loss
The Spirit of Her Being
To weep by a cross

The Hour of Angels
The mysteries they cry
Solemn the moon
In a Contemplating Sky

Streams watch mountain rainstorms
To regard how they run
The shadows of the night time
As they wait for the sun

A candle as it burns
In the stillness of the night
The flame beside a prayer…
The luminosity of its light.

Maybe

Maybe, I am 'dead'
But I'm only 'alive'
And to question the natures
It takes to survive.

His Shadow

...the Winter's dominions – celestial
Airs are tranquil and calm
My hand collects from the Angels
As snow falls on my palms

I regard from a bay window
A scene like the veil of a bride
The thought of him haunts my longing
And my heart, in the room where I hide

Each time the snows would grace the grounds
I remember us again
The midnight, we met in the Temple
And how I loved your vein

When tears fall from the heavens
In their frozen ethereal state...
Just as love is eternal
So the reasons that you were my fate...

A light as it enters my soul
I know that he is there
His presence brings a warmth to my soul
Emotions emblazon the air

His... a mystical world
Candles tend... to roar
He leads me down a hallway and through a hidden door

The castle that lives in the winter
Perfect, the snows as they glisten
An Angel watches over the scene
You can see, if you listen

A lingering euphoria
My eyes as they widen – I yearn as he nears
The quietness of the room
As he tenderly kisses my tears

Mirrors and roses
A candle's aurora, the room
A ring rests in some ice
Our souls beneath a radiant moon

The castle that lives in the winter
The snows as they glisten
An Angel watches over the scene
You can see… if you listen.

The Playground

A victim as I cried
Did You hear the sound?
Memories left
From an 'Educational' playground

When ghosts play in the storms
The grounds as they tell
The way that people make a place
For, skies that know the memory well

How one takes breath
And shadows as they dare
The grounds beneath my soles
The grounds… regard their cares…

And if life is not fair, Maybe
Man made it such
For that which gave us freedom
To ask for too much?

The spirits of a playground,
Still, some can't play?
And ways to remember
The night and the day

The Law of a heart
What man dares to break (it)?
Though the nature of Love
I'd still not forsake it.

People are children
I gaze into the river
A mirror knows it's Son
A Sacred Sky – the mirror.

The Letter

A cold anamnesis
A haunting from the past
Memories to my soul
Closed in on me fast

Would I have known
What would plan my tomorrows
I'd have stayed in the shadows
Away from these sorrows

Tears run though tables may turn
As if a weary heart may wish to learn…
A smile… a sanction
An interaction

A place
Where all that remains
Of historical pains
Are skies of sound dreaming
And love

A cold anamnesis
A haunting from the past
Memories to my soul
Closed in on me fast…

Another Place and Time in November

This place is tranquil
This place is still
And I'm still alive
I know for I'm ill.

And lonely is 'funny'
For who could have thought
That life was a lesson
And such things were taught

And heartbroken summer
The sun as it burns
And colder the winter
But when will they learn?

Life is so simple
It's all black and white
One can't turn back the time
So they did what was not right

Cruel desolation
And ongoing fight
That haunts at the soul
Between darkness and light

'Foreign' the Sundays
What could condone?
A heart as it breaks
When there's no place like home

For all of this life
It never was mine
And would 'shadows' always worry me
Till the end of time.?

And Skies as they seem
As the darkness takes it's time
If God was really watching
How? the devil had crime?

And am I worth saving
When it rains once again?
I try to recall the time when I last smiled
But I can't remember when

The nadir of a day
The moon and what's done
When things are as such
And there's no place like home

Something You Said
The Ring

And there is nowhere to go...
So to ever run for cover?
To wonder of life,
"For I was not another"

This world, sometimes absurd
What rests behind eyes…
For the Mirror of one's Soul.
Where the Son of the Skies?

Nothing here seems real
Neath the dark and stormy clouds
Candles flicker on a chandelier
The empty skies ring loud

A woman's slavery, a marriage and such witness
Every moon before
To harm so much a freedom
The haunting at the door.

The grounds of a day…
Before the wreckage of another
A dulling hurt – another's land
I had no witness other

And to regard from the balcony
In the shadows neath the moon
Where nights are not for dreaming
And morning comes too soon.

Beneath the evidence of suns and moons…
Still the watch of prayers
Though despite the sands of time…
The things that still dare to a morrow.

The world of 'Absurd'
When the sun stares into eyes
The Mirror of the Soul
Where the Son of the Skies?

Demanding dejection
An era's Sunday and it's shame
A cold Pandora's Box
The years given to pain.

Grey the scene that mimes from the window
A soporific sky
Suffocating panes
And a life of alibi.

To ever cry for help
And there is nowhere to go
So to ever lose the mind
Until there's nothing left to know

A crime against innocence
A deed against the sky
The river as it echoes
A lonely alibi

His Haunting Madrigal – Elegy

When the day was dark
And shadows fell to tainting
The ' vein ' of his skin argued
Like the mystery in a painting

And now, to regard a piano
In the stillness of a room
At least the keys are black and white
Would they take away the gloom

To wonder of life
What… one speaks of another
To gaze into the river

To wonder of words…
When one 'is not another'.

Yes… people make a place
And life it should be fair
But the sentences that punish
The cross that some must bear

Dangerous liaisons
One am alone
The Angels know (when) a day's "curtain down"
Yet... to love the Skies they own.

Rains... as they sob
Perhaps, they take to grieving
Bah… Bah… black sheep…
The song that sometimes skies they sing

In a world that's so sublime
The pilgrims and the swallows
To recall wherever he goes
An Angel always follows.

An Unkindness of 'Heavens' –
The Blackness of Ravens

The day as it passes
To live to tell…
If the good die young,
They've chosen well…

War and Hospitality – To Be Attracted to Leaving

I had 'lost' my way
And hell is always such, that
To know too little is a dangerous thing
And yet… to know too much

Was I attracted to leaving…
But they threw me to their floor
Angers as they stared
Their hatreds barred the door

The realm of that dance
Sundays, and their doom
My hurt – I was provoked
And the day was gone too soon

The 'denials' neath their warring heavens
Memories as they loom
I would miss you in the silence
My anxieties in that room

Interrogations… heartbeats
Ever to 'assume'
For, when another plays with sorrows
I (had) 'turned' about them in that room

Silent and unholy war
The hells within that sand
My soul thrown… To a desert
For I now danced in the wrong land

Weary of the grounds
The cold anthem and it's ways
The music as it played
In the heartlessness of days

Disturbed the shadows in restless storms
And skies, for they would stare
To look unto the rain until
No solace could be there

The shadows to my skin
My heart within my 'crime'
The skies became estranging
The 'dance' become a mime

To ever tell the truth to them?
How skies would be ill
So, the shadows of a wreckage
By a tired window sill.

The Minks

The minks as they cry out, and play in the mere
They shake the water from their coats...I catch a 'tear.'

Moonlight Serenade

In the days that breathe without you
Each yesterday a morrow
This 'ornamental' sanity
To while away the sorrow

Aloneness broods the night
In the mazes of the dark
A world of many masquerades
'Alone in Noah's Ark'

I look into a crowd
Yet I know you won't be there
My heart undone to cry
The moonlight soft… on the midnight air.

I pretend that you are with me
The world sent me to sigh
The ways that I would miss you
Beneath the Sacred Sky.

A slave to know love lost
Yet still I took that chance
I wander in the rain
Where the Angels always dance

The way that love can give and take
It's profuse, commanding law
This night… to sense as though winter
Had ravaged my 'core'

In a room, my hands would trace the walls
This prison and it's yearn
The shadows now you're gone
The solitude that learns me.

As the moon believes the earth
It circles to a prayer
The room keeps on spinning
The heartaches as they dare

The Mind Behind Your Kiss

Summer as it dyes the grounds
The tea rose in my hand
The mind behind your kiss
And how you tell me that I am

Midnight turns to morning
And we are left alone
My heart's attention turns to your lips
The things that they condone

Gentle his manner
Compelling … his touch
The skies as they submit to night
His nature…

Horizons as they echo
The storms by which we race
The lightening hits the rivers
Your heartbeat as I pace

Reasons as you kiss me
The way that I am taken
In the juries of a sky
My guard is 'forsaken'

For you are one in a million
And you are one of a kind
The night as it passes
And memories flood my mind.

Blues

The melody as it plays
Would it colour the room
The keys as they sound
To take away the gloom

To awaken in another's 'dream'
Exploitations and oppressions
Apartheids… shallow causes
The slaves that were deemed possessions.

To serve the self is not slavery
To not ever question why
Take a gander at the heavens
And the reasons to cry

Sunday and gloomy
And whose mocking and token?
Damning the damned
And breaking the broken

To ever chose what to learn in life?
So, the pain as it raves…
To watch the flowers
That grow about unmarked graves.

When the sloth of heart inspires
Hurts to be played
Hands when they tremble
What do they fear?

To love the tears of the Blue
To walk and sing neathe their rain
To feel in Law and reason
To know in happiness and pain

the follies of a day (to break in laws)
Injured "many a scene"
To ever care to plot a morrow
A hurt that has been

For such a place is cold
And yesterdays leave their stain
To take another breath that way…
What have you to gain?

Searching

Sometimes, 'dark – my understanding of the world
Though, beneath the skies am I
To wonder of the things that be…
Lugubrious the hours… that I sigh for.

Winter's storms as they glare through me…
I'm searching for a sanity
A peace from the pain
Where heartbreaks don't reign

I walk the sleepless city searching
For my fate to elevate
Hope fades away
Evanescing day

Unbroken Falls
(In Relating to the War
and Psychiatric Abuse)

Foreign asylum
Just like a curse
'Anathemas' as they linger
The shadow of the nurse.

For a slave trade nursed it's child
And such was also the war
To not wonder of a heartlessness
Or any corner's broken Law.

Patients dragged back screaming
Through a weighted door
Elsewhere, a soldier drags a beaten man
To question him more

Anxious the nights
Until nothing will calm
To tell untruths of one in a 'coma'
The discountenance, as skies watch in alarm.

Borderlines… occupations
Where? was the jest?
How they laugh at another's war dead
And what happened to the rest?

The old asylum off "Church lane"
To herd them just like… cattle
Spirits as they stir there
Accusations as they 'rattle'

To pride the self with patients
Orchids made of plastic
The war… it's sordid and hollow goad.
The doctor of it …low and sarcastic.

To look back on a past
Am I falling from a height…
To report 'the 'cattle' are lowing?!'
To grant themselves what right?!

Comatose awareness
Each heartbreak and its phase
To throw to hell another's world
So that hell contrives the days

Diplomacies… hospitalities
Sarcastic… as they tore at the dead
To deny everything that ever lived
And all they ever said

Of countless missing shadows
I sat to mourn a while
The subtleties that undermine in a room
Could I not live in denial

Minutes pass so slowly
A clock as it would tick
War transgressions and despairs…
How they always make me sick…

To tell me every Sunday
Night skies are always black
To break… to mourn again
For all that wars would lack

For failing to say 'Madagascar'
The silent treatment and scoff
War crimes and reminiscences
Hearts as they beat in their cold, baleful sloth

The psychology of some 'heavens'
Were they pitiless to save
The quietness as I wept was marred…
The 'screaming' of their hatreds through graves…

And the memory as it echoes in my head
Through the dead and lost dreams
And I regard the mask of the stillness
Though all is not as it seems

Storms as they crash
Their angers as stated
Spirits as they dance
And that which is Sacred.

Sadistic… the 'play'
A sordid masquerade
The darkness… where it hides…
…the strangest escapade

To Ever Make A Killing

Scorns within the Playground
The Sky above the time
The battle in the heavens
The one the people mime

Motions seem surreal
The conservation of genocide
How the war can cast a nation
To wonder by what god they abide?

No storybooks, no fairytales
But to sabotage an age
The writing on the wall
To the writings on a page

People to their death sentence
The intrigues of a failure
The supremacies of darkest ways
Settled then the
Savior?

For, to acknowledge the power of what?
The devil and its charge?
So hindmost, a bad dream…
Or is it all a 'joker's mirage'?

The mindscapes of a chaos
What 'sanities'! Of man?
Souls wake in a twisted dream…
And a world's hypocritical damn?

How political 'the doctor'
And how! A land would love a neighbour
The years that they do nothing
But cause trouble and it's labour

The Golden Gardens

The way souls wished in yesterdays
Yet, to live without regret
What is left to say?
Some dance to remember… some dance, to forget.

To kneel by the oceans and pray,
In the golden gardens of yearning
The tears that echo the ages
The effulgent sun, softly burning

Let us bide the midnight there
Until darkness turns to light
And let God plan our morrow
The wonders of His might.

I Hear Him in the Winter...

The fall of the snows
And the dusk as he cries
The mysteries of love
And conundrums of skies.

And the Summer Rains

His mazing mind – the maze
Amazing mind.
The haze.
His 'amusing' muse in the mews
And to cave in to the news as he kissed me in the stables.
My mazing mind not to mind at all
X

Of Sunday

Sardonic 'war and peace and... war'
Shadows pointed blame
The guns, like hell as bodies fell
And souls shocked... for 'their gain'

That hell that always tries
To ravage through 'the 'dreams'
Vultures and their conscience
Would they 'enquire' for their 'underworld'

Nocturnal patrols and slayings
Darker yet, the nights
The stars would fade from distraction
Gun smoke and it's plights.

Night times as slaveries
'Paranoias' as they loom
The people in the village
Each 'wrong breath' in each 'wrong room'

Monotonous oblivions
Inertias and their doom
That plotted in the silence
Neath a deafening moon

The lawlessness in the morning
As the wicked claimed for more
I not 'sober' from the nightmare
My soul left on the floor

Tell the Suns

And 'callous' the war… the fires of the sun
The flames as if to revel
For when war buys man's brain then heart
Would it go but save the devil.

When deeds are there to kill…
Deceptions and irreligion
The dysphoria and social battles on a land
(Beside) each political 'circus' and decision.

To injure a morning,
And scarlet the skies that they hurt
For storms, the skies can change…
So to ever save a shirt.

Life is…
So to not wonder of the price
To allow in war and witness once
To ever know it happens twice

"Disempowering"… to the soul
And maybe I'm naive?
But another's paroxysm and suffer
Why would that relieve you?

For the political 'April fools' to learn
And the scenes that they would mask
And memories are irreplaceable
Each sufferance… and it's task.

The way a hell can laugh the heart
Shadows as they gain
A field of 'flatlines' and reveries
Until sullen with pain.

In counts of morrows and each yesteryear
A 'high-wire' as it racks
Lifelessness imitates an artful war
For the heart the devil lacks

Oaths and Sides

The world keeps on turning
The room and it's learning
When fires are burning
A Saturnine Saturn's rings.

The sound of the shadows
As they circle a room
The earth as it turns
And storms about the moon

The lake cast frozen
Beneath the nebulous skies
The ice as it shatters
When lightning 'sighs'.

The 'Blue' may it mind me
The moon and it's 'Reich'
For one cannot love
What they don't even like

Knowing is knowing
And memories remain
the nature of the Truth
Would always stay the same

Spectres and Shadows

Unnatural days
So; long live the hatred'?
Spectres and shadows
Where 'Nothing' is Sacred.

And 'Nothing ' in common
Neath the rains as they fall
And eyes when they stare
Are 'Nothing ' at all

For war means… to mar the era
(For) 'evil doppelganger' scenes
Until the living are the dead
And any town is left without dream.

A fool's highest heaven…
The war and it's 'hat trick'
To fear the line of the 'lost'
To then 'go to cross it'?!

The shadows of their deeds
Until the skies become irate
To ever vomit at the table of
The devil incarnate.

Leave out (the Known)
And ('’not ours to judge')
So
The seen and the unseen
Rains as they fall

Memories of dying…
To consider them all.

The String Quartet – Bad Dream

To look out from the balcony
The moon… and it's beam
The suns as they rest
Are not what they seem here.

Nine o clock November
I'm lying on the floor
The cold airs as I shudder
In this room without a door

The beatings in their pounds
A string quartet was playing
The soldiers on their rounds
The background for their slaying.

I can't seem to move…
Silence …as I'm trying to scream…
And the struggle… as it mocks me
Like an unsound dream

In the dead of the night
The discontentment won't cease
It preys in the silence
For the pieces of the peace

I close my eyes in the darkness…
Unknowns and their strife
This comatose hell
And parallel life

And I've only one prayer
And am I worth saving?
It rains from the Sky
It reigns from its Graveness and Haven.

With You

Sundays on the land with you…
The warmth of December
You are always with me…
And do I always remember

When I fell into your arms
In shades of night and day….
The numberless ways…
You took my breath away

Paint Me a Place

Paint me a place
Where the minutes pass the test of vice
Show me a case
Where the hour is not reflecting a price
Give me a day
There is not a knife in a back to twist
Take me away
To where a need never goes unmissed

Paint me a face
That does not conjure a smile to deceive (me)
Find me a race
Of storms that can set me a pace
Show me a heart
That is connected to the hand I shake
And the Heart that is whole and true…
…As it watches a day break

(Poem From 'Russian Midnights' – 2014)

Alien skies, Mourning doves Till all I can do Is… think of your gloves.

Graves and shadows
The tears to his soul – And, reasons why his heart would sigh
For the Law above his dole

His manner to my heart
Would it learn me to behave
Something of his hand
The way in which it saves me

What I believe… and that which is true – to love you past the ends of time, (Is)
A thing I always knew
And Seconds go so slowly – Then the minutes fade away – And, 'no such thing
as time' – For, The ours to a day
The beat of your heart – The way that I land – Forgive me, I fell – Thus, the scar
on your hand
To see what you believe
With the mirrors of your soul
And the way he looked upon me
Beneath the falling rains
A fathomless love – For where shadows are from – My thoughts of you
through… The days that have gone
Darkness as it calls The sun, the sky to leave The tears of a candle Our love as it
breathes
The enigmas of our shadows – Sundown as it dyes – the horizons as colours fall
across – Alien skies
Your world as it revolves My spirit as it turns Angels dawn the skies And Our
candle as it yearns
In the shadows, the way of us The mystery you bear You enter a room… I know
that you are there
And how you touch the silence – As night falls from day – The nature of your
presence, The room, it fades away
The storms as they bawl sometimes, the beating of my heart… The shadows that
haunt me
You tear them apart
My name in your presence You know I forget To ever goodbye you?
My heart would not let

Pinocchios and Feathers
The Windmills of a Mind

So forlorn, to face the consequences... I went to the Pawn-brokers.
Foreign hospitality… No sobre lawyer was to be found
Where not only paintings hang…
And Casanovas shout in rounds

Eyes as they acclimatize
Breaches as they revel
There's 'something in the water'
To need a "holiday in Seville".

What windmill? And…a pebble?
Someone tosses in a stream?!
Thus, no refuge by a wishing well
Or any fairytale or dream

Escape their "lusty shopping sprees"
Sarcastic Cavaliers
Where the prosecution's witness?
The poe leece? (police)
"Swingers"? on the chandeliers

"Pinocchio's 'Geronimos'
Till there's no hotel room to trust
Yes Yes – 'paroqueets' etc.
And therefore, somewhat rusty (of manner).

His bulldog as it 'jogs'
And so the nature of 'panting' !
To wonder of someone's Sinbads"
The sky of much ranting

Dogs with quotidien dogma
Dogpaddling ' in the sea
Why not 'pussyfooting pusillanimously '
Beneath their father's willow tree.

I was not an 'Il'
And the mind gets somewhat listless
A man can have 1000 '(ro)bots'
But his 'language' would still use a mistress…?

Like chimpanzees ! as they imitate
A 'round of broken hearts'
Nymphomania cowboys… moving sex bots…
The bull herd as it darts !

A bazaar of aphrodisiacs
An old game, old heart breaker
Deceivers and broken hearts
Man's coldest dream taker

To go to the dogs' as philanderers
And sleeping dogs for they lie
ACHT HUNDERT pfund und ras'cals
For a malefactor and his 'fly'!

Is this the bit where I come in with

"A feather for every wind that blows"?

"No… you're late…"

Escape their kiss of "lurve" !
Sarcastic Cavaliers
Narcotics und those… philistines !
"Swinging"?! from the chandeliers

Aspect

"A gloomy love of literature
Sundays as they think
They only harm the
Spirit
But not the one they drink

My heart beats me for longer
The unknowns of this game
The 'colours' of a candle
The sun would see it's flame."

"The war as it raves
the core of its lies
The injections they forced
To my arms before my eyes"

The demons neath the 'skin' of war
An ill 'default' and hatred
To disrespect all that
Another holds Sacred.

And… prisoners of war…
Shadows as they cower
Immorality and decadence…
Anathemas as they tower.

For, the nature of arms
And weapons of war
An injection in monies…
For another Law… to be broken

Asylums and wars
For madness (is) a sin
A place of no God
"Where have you been?"

A pain that is 'mine not your's'
To hear quite well … but true?
For, what you do not know – It cannot hurt you?
When I Behave

'Burned'

Heartless the day
It must be a crime
A candle as it burns…
'What is yours is mine'

This eerie 'sedation'…
The loneliness as it towers
And am I exhausted
Monotonous the hours

Like dust that gathers in a room…
And how I am 'worn'.
The earth as it circles beneath the sky
In The screaming of the poltergeist storm

And am I always ill?
The grounds' memory of many moons and suns,
And The world keeps on turning…
Until cruel the river as it runs

Wry nightmare… wry
In the falling rain
To regard my own breath
Our reasons ever the same?

What of dreams?
Alien skies and cruel
When happiness hath politic
A mechanic hath a tool

The Way that I Dream
A Salzburg Moon

Are the wonders they speak of the grounds, but true
And so… the nature of love
Shadows as they dare
Before the skies above.

A heart as it beats
And love hath it's power
The way that I dream
Alone in my bower

Abandons that Cast Grounds to Sorrow

Day…for it passes
This night as I walk in the rain
The moon as it hangs in a desert of skies…
The moon… as it's waning.

To ever be careless of Skies
Abandons that cast grounds to sorrow
I listen to the shadows
The sleeplessness journeys tomorrow.

The Circus of the War

The circus of the war
A bitter masquerade
Enemies' hatreds
The music as it plays

Colloquial the manner
Political the tease
The thought chains beneath unholy wars
So to anthem that 'disease'

In another hundred years…
To ask of where I sat?
In the jury of my injuries
Where was the jest in that?

When politic is heartless
Tyrannical the mind
And deadlines as they shroud the days
A sin would lead the blind

The world and it's forgiven
For each morrow's yesterday
Yet the dead that shadows leave
Somehow, they'll never go away

Slaughtering rains…
A nightmare as it winds
Gunfire and haggled souls
The hauntings of a mind

Enemies' hatreds?
Do friends render worse?
Wrong places and times
A war and it's curse

A lifetime of emotions
The angles of their crime
(For),What commands the soul
When one cannot turn back the time?

To predate on each mourning
The skies of shameless face
The way that they try deny
The sadness of the case

The grounds were ever safe
Beside the sins of man?
The confessions of the war
"To wonder what I am".

Wednesday's Midnight Skies – The Dance
(Loosely Inspired By Nijinsky)

Tired eyes and wounded soul
The marring scenes again
Would not a Saint dwell to a heart
Beside a River Seine?

The core of the soul
As though the devil sieged alms
To fall apart… to fall apart
A heart haunted by Psalms

From the work of iron will
As though an agony went unheard
To question any conscience… or
The nature of the world

Patronizing sentences
– their recidivist… stare
And the lunar above frustrations
That echo every air

And the world keeps on turning
Like a strange alien wheel
Beneath a seeking 'clay pot'
A heart condemned to feel

When December knows tears
In the depth of each
Nocturne
How a minute goes so slowly
The pain as it could learn one

To prescribe "a pity of yesters"
To ever feel or know
Until the memories are lost
In the religion of the snow…

And poetry in motion
In the cold, nostalgic haze

For "Is it in Heaven somewhere
… the mirror of His days."

A desert's forty nights and it's voices
But men's prisons and a 'waiter'
God before the name of him
Judged by his Creator

The exiles of a dance
The asylums they forgot
Sometimes a prayer, it hurts,
Sometimes it hurts one not.

And at midnight how the world
Gets over its tomorrow
Though yesterday is near
When suns don't dry the sorrow

And when ignorance is near,
Who suffers for its bliss
For what he didn't know
To hurt like this…

A freedom that is given and
The prison and the 'waiter'
God before the name of him
Judged by his Creator

Drowning

Foreign asylum
For man's law was psychiatric
To know that hell could shroud law
It's mind of vile hat trick

Lonely my life
Frustrations as they prey
To goodbye the darkness
But it carries to day…

To drown in doctored truths
My spirit as it sunk
A painting, or patient as they hung
But the witness must have drunk

Suicides… oppressive politics
The 'side effects' were dear
In a hell no one sees
And no one can hear

Violent the shadows
Paintings and frames
To ever shame hearts?
The Blood in His veins.

"I thought that this was this way"
The file as it changed
The way they doctored notes
Was I more and more estranged

Was it a game?
The People in pain?
When a Sky would tell them
Desist!
The way devils resist the Maker's Sanities

Antitheses madness
Unholy the wars
They go pay the devil
Till they die for its cause

Downward spirals
The cause of their thinking
A war's doctored files and their sands
To watch the self sinking

What God in the skies?!
And how the skies burn
To dance by the Neva
But the day as it turned.

Sombre my mind
Freedom and it's legacy
Rains as they woe,
Their pathetic… pathetic fallacy

The Era

Another shattered heart
Delirious with pain
The devil breaks the spirit
The world resounds its bane

The nightmare as it reels
A monster's virulent deed
The politics of hell
The shadows of its creed

Seagulls screech 'cross 'poltergeist' skies
The halls as patients scream
Nothing be there to calm the graves
In the "house of unsound dream"

Opium and sorrows' wars
Matter… and its core
The vultures in the shadows
And… prisoners of war

The coldest of psychologies
The 'doctor' knew reverse
A book of how to starve the soul
Assisted by a curse!

And all the world's a madhaus and
Sunday's asylum
The 'damned' and 'conveniently'
misdiagnosed
The 'doctor' paid to sigh them

The skies in their slow motions
The way they're always sober
But the tortures without conscience
Do their Sunday lies grow older.

And faces become strangers
After the 'cruel' and the dead
The nature of that 'orphanage'
The way that things were said

The coldest hospitality
What the 'teacher' that takes a life
The hell of hells lesson to learn
The 'Back' that bleeds from each knife

And undulating hell
And days without a truth

Where (be) the Heart that beats behind the 'Vault', (ref. Vault of the Skies)
For, each breath and so, it's proof.

The nightmare as it reels
A monster's virulent deed
The politics of hell
The shadows of its creed

A night of candle vigils
The Angels as they follow
Fires as they flicker
The way they laugh and sorrow.

33 Decembers

And 33 Decembers
Did I wander them about
The 'Fragile'… of the world
And no easy way out.

When the Dead Seas mirror the heavens
Nebulous night, and long way the fall
When God finds children missing
Is it lonely at all…?

Let not the people turn their backs
On the Sky that cast them here
Does it seem that breath is far
(but) God is always near

Would Heaven guard a soul
And cry for all its hurt
For wounds as they would weep
From the Back beneath a 'shirt' of
Blue Skies.

And loneliness Is strange
When all is done and said
When you believe in that which 'Lives'
For you cannot that which is 'dead'.

If all the world's a stage…
Each Beautiful 'part'
The lunars as they pass
Their knowing and their
Art

In the Dark to Spend My Time

Dark the skies this night
With him, they seem kind
And is it everything at all –
As I find myself attracted…

He traces my palms
Neath the moons of his world
To hold me in his arms

Beneath the roaring skies…
Curious a flame
To yield to the fire
Where love alone is to blame

In the jury of my senses
His shadow to my heart
In the realms of emotion
The angles to his art

For all the heart can say
Does love sigh it's mime
To lay to rest my guard
In the dark, to spend my time

The moons as they circle the earth
What dictates the beat of a heart?
How he knows my being
How I love my part

The sky of aurora
Our shadows compete
Rebellions roar the silence
Am I 'defeated'

Colours cross the heavens
Emotions as they call
The many ways to love
In the shadows of the fall.

So I Tend to Believe

And weary I am
From the 'clouds' and their ways
As I journey through time
And regard all my days.

The colours of the Blue
Why should they care?
A problem… a conundrum
Will it always be there?

It strikes me that I'm beaten
For I can't work it out
A problem shared is a problem doubled
For I have asked about…

Sometimes of joy
(It's) "Like a loan for a day"
To wait for the world
To take it away

And weary I am
From 'Claudes' and their ways
As I journey through time
And "regard" all my days.

When troubles want more
And crazy the days
Life as it tries one
In the craziest ways

I look to the skies
How they always have time
And something out there tells me
"It always was Mine"
Though, when I do get things
Right… Does it ever relieve?
Isaac Newton my apple!
Though I tend to believe.

Meet Me on a Sunday

Meet me on a Sunday
The swing neath the tree
And when we're playing kiss chase
I hope you're after me

If we should to 'hide and seek'
I shan't say where I am
For if you were to find me
You'd be an honest man

On the Rocks

A drink and its hat trick
The drunk and confused
The glass as it stares
'til some eyes are bemused.

To ever sell a puppet to souls
To regard the way they 'sway'
To watch as they harm themselves or another
A fiendish hangover to pay

The memories that dwell
Neath a psychedelic's façade
The night as it falls
When the lunar seems marred

Blurred and headache the surroundings
'Influence and under'
Estranging how – the mind and the body
Belong to 'another'.

Actions are souls…
The piano as it played
The hours as they passed
Until night fell to day.

For if hearts beat to temptations
(And) denials of crimes are against the sky
To regard the storms in the skies
And a lonely alibi.

Take for instance… your life
The shadows that gazed
And which drink cast those sarcastic
Blue murder days

10 green bottles
The miasma of brutes
I was driving my soul
To escape their pursuits

To yearn to be farther
Another 'job' and 'education' done
The fool of those days
And next, the 'remembrance sun'.

Empty

The 'asylums' of diablo
The circles of the war
The prisons that they hide…
What arms beneath their law

So many natures to the questioning
And their 'storms' would lend to kicking
The water as I choked
The clock as it was ticking

The water that they forced
The madness of its role
The air for which I thirsted
To throw 'the desert'… to my soul

And soul destroying torture…
Carmine and bloody…
Aspects of politic
The heartless egos that were 'fed' there.

The beatings in their 'pounds'
The music was playing
Henchmen on their rounds
The background for their slaying

The 'empty' bays of diablo
A wicked disdain
The tarnish and torture
And skies would send their rain

The skies – the vault of their entity
The solace that they give
A man can tell a thousand truths
And so, the right to live

The bays of diablo
The prisons of the war
Man serves his mind's asylum
The thought chains beneath a Law.

The Hurricane

When skies are weary of sleeping
And I don't need the dreams
Life is not to me
What every day seems to be here

And it is not the hurt
But the loneliness I cannot bear
To be lost in each silence
In the middle of a 'nowhere'

When the Sky has its heartaches
Written on a sleeve
To know the nature of Your being
If I listen as I breathe

To Miss You – Come Home

No December with you
No February rains
To wonder what is left of my heart
And what leaves breath through my veins

Am I so Dreamless from sorrows…
Would the skies sense my tears if
They were wept before the blind
And beside 'one who cannot hear'

Restless the night
Until nothing can calm
Shadows as they beckon me to
The fires of the gardens

I journey through the labyrinth
The luminous moon
On the tree swing, I sway
And dream of a summer June…

Hours as I long for you…
For given to remember
Though, to say that I must know
Another cold December

When midnight heavens… regard one's eyes…
And there's just too much 'blue'.
This fire as it burns…
What it is to miss you

A heart as it beats
And your being haunts my mind
Memories of you…
The hours they unwind…

Passions as they 'torture' me
When love knows to be free
Sometimes loneliness is a friend
But even that needs company

In the moonlight, I lament…
Shadows watch me gravely
Would the mind of the heavens…
Have mercy to save me…

The Probable Consequences

In the gothic garden
And how, I love your blood
Have I loved you in 'evers'
Memories as they flood

You kiss me… for an answer…
The probable consequence
Our beings in the shadows
As you take down my defenses

And night time is our playground
The mystery where we 'hide'
The things to do before the oceans,
And the stories of the tide.

Skies watch the roses yearn
As they wait for the rain
The art of their 'sadism'
The pleasure of your vein.

The mystery in your eyes
My weakness for your hand
And to love to fear the things
I do not understand.

Forever and for Love

I gravitate to you
And do I like the way…
You catch my hand…
And tell me to stay…

Your embrace neath the rains
How you soothe my 'cry'…
My breath in your arms
…the storms as they sigh

The way that you hold me
And… render my part
I am given to liking you
And the nature of your 'art'

Your way with me…
And I am for you
Forever, and for love…
And how you tell me that it's true…

This Love

In a room of many mirrors
As candles cajole
The chambers of his heart
Gently stir a soul

His hand as she sighs
Each moment to reminisce
He circles her and seeks
For the memory of a kiss

The sky above their tempers
Thunders as they roll
He searches her eyes
And renders her dole

Their shadows as they motion
In a beautiful game
The way in which a heart beats
In a place where love's to blame

He regards her intently…
The night and its sound
Her necklace bears his ring
Scarlet roses on the ground

His nature… his intention
Where knowing is only this
The silence of his vow
In the 'sinews' of his kiss

The reflections of a candle
It's warm and sacred flame
Snows as they fell in ages gone by
Love's unbending truth remains…

The religion of his soul
As the moon burns above Emotions
and their shadows… *This love*

Before His Back

When my heart is with you
Passion and her fire
To take a 'Book' and read
And of you, I cannot tire

Your soul stirs my senses
And whilst gentle, your way
Your 'force' leads me to buckle
As I warm to what you say

And each day learns my eyes
Am I, 'susceptible' to you
To know one's own shadow
To know another's too

The nature of soul
That dwells beneath your eyes
I am safe with you
Beneath forbidding skies

And when you touch my hands
Neath the skies, as if to pray
The feeling that I'd know
For I'd sense what he would say

Beneath the rains, he holds my being
I rest in his embrace
To sense the man I love
Be such… my favoured place.

The power of Love
The undeniable 'attack'
And I love him when he looks upon me
So too, before his back.

Eternal

The Sacred Book of Heaven
And the grounds that deem her sky
To be unafraid
For Love, cannot die.

Tango

A passion without words
A dance and its 'muse'
Persuasive how you motion
To resist you, would I lose

Elegant confessions
And midnight's cue
The substance of a man
The fortitude of you

The longing that hides in a dance
Emotion overwhelms
Figures in the darkness
Your breath about my realms

The music as it changes
And your lips are gone too soon
The hungers of a fire
Neath the essence of the moon.

Forbidden… and through the night with you
Beneath the fires of the sky
The music and its escapade
The dance that we sigh.

If Each Deed Is a Prayer

The storms as they learn…
A desert's restless… sands
The rains would not stop falling
As I went to 'wash' my hands

Do the Angels serve each other
Is the world a spinning room
Do rainfalls dye the forest grounds…
And the flowers bloom

Would I bathe my hair, December
Before the picture of a Saint
If each thought or deed is a prayer,
A picture as it's 'painted'.

The Vault of the Heavens to learn
The grounds and their loss
It's sacred meditation
As He 'passed' on the cross

And, 33 Decembers
Has there always been a Law
And Love sees not only with the eye
And I know You knew before.

To believe, in the religion… of peace,
And the morning… the reasons it grieves…
Fearlessness can be, a dangerous game
The skin on the soul of the sky, as it breathes

For the dreams that rest in eyes
And wonders of the times
Prayers unto the heavens
The shadows and their 'mimes'.